T0118864

Milet Publishing
Smallfields Cottage, Cox Green
Rudgwick, Horsham, West Sussex
RH12 3DE England
info@milet.com
www.milet.com
www.milet.co.uk

First English–Russian edition published by Milet Publishing in 2013

Copyright © Milet Publishing, 2013

ISBN 978 1 84059 782 0

Original Turkish text written by Erdem Seçmen
Translated to English by Alvin Parmar and adapted by Milet

Illustrated by Chris Dittopoulos
Designed by Christangelos Seferiadis

All rights reserved. No part of this publication may be reproduced in any form or
by any means without the written permission of the publishers.

Printed and bound in Turkey by Ertem Matbaası

My Bilingual Book

Hearing
Слух

English–Russian

Our ears are like our radar

Как радары наши уши,

for hearing sounds from far.

Чтобы далеко и близко слушать.

Our ears delight in hearing shouts of glee.

Нам звуки ликования ласкают слух.

I am happy for you, and you are happy for me.

С победой поздравлять мы рады всех вокруг!

Do you hear that buzz? Oh no . . .

Слышишь этот тонкий писк?

It's a mosquito!

Комар летает вверх и вниз!

The sweet voice of my mother

Нежный голос моей мамы

is a sound like no other.

Во всем мире лучший самый!

Hearing is a very sensitive sense.

Мы звуки слышим. Если ж звуки не слышны,

We hear sounds and also silence.

Попробуй уловить звучанье тишины.

When there's too much noise,

Так много шума здесь вокруг!

it's hard to hear one voice.

Непросто различить, что скажет друг.

I hear the sound of propellers, so I know

Я слышу шум пропеллера и знаю,

it's a traffic helicopter, flying low.

Что это вертолет над нашим домом пролетает.

If we could listen to music all day long,

Ах, если б слушать целый день, как музыка звучит!

we would learn the words to every song!

Могли б слова мы каждой песни заучить!

Our ears are for hearing what's around us,

Наши уши нужны, чтобы слушать –

and also for listening to what's inside us.

И то, что внутри нас, и то, что снаружи.

Morning brings a happy noise,

Нам утро звуки счастья принесет, –

the sound of birds chirping, singing their joys!

Щебечут птицы, и душа поет!